ANIMAL
COLORS

A Rainbow of Colors from Animals
Around the World

ANIMAL
COLORS

A Rainbow of Colors from Animals
Around the World

Beth Fielding

EarlyLight Books

Waynesville, North Carolina, USA

Cataloging Information

Fielding, Beth.
    Animal colors: A rainbow of colors from animals around the world/ Beth Fielding
       32 p. : ill. ; 23 cm.
    Summary: Explores the colors found in animals from a range of taxa. Includes
          information on the uses of color in animals, such as camouflage for
          predators and prey, and advertisement to attract mates and warn
          predators. Also includes conservation and behavior information.
    LC: QL 767
    Dewey: 591.4
    ISBN-13: 978-0-9797455-4-6 (alk. paper)
    ISBN-10: 0-9797455-4-3 (alk. paper)
          Animals – Color – juvenile literature.

Art Director: Stewart Pack
Photo Production: Kimberly Pack
Project Editor: Dawn Cusick
Copy Editor: Susan Brill

10 9 8 7 6 5 4 3 2 1

First edition

Published by EarlyLight Books, Inc.
1436 Dellwood Road
Waynesville, NC 28786

Copyright © 2009 EarlyLight Books, Inc.

Distributed by BookMasters, Inc.

Manufactured in China.
All rights reserved.

ISBN 13: 978-0-9797455-4-6
ISBN 10: 0-9797455-4-3

To Julianna Rose
May your life be filled with colo

Contents

Red

Turkey
Males call to females by saying gobble-gobble or cluk-cluk; has no feathers on face; raccoons like to eat its eggs and babies

Red Rooster

Wakes up people with a loud song every morning; the red crest on top of its head is called a comb; funny thing under its chin is called a wattle

Lobster

Lives on sandy bottom of ocean floor; uses antennae to smell; related to spiders and bugs; can have 100 birthdays (but doesn't get cake and candles!)

Red-Spotted Salamander

Hunts for bugs and spiders for food; babies live in water; teenagers live in the woods; adults live in mud; poison on its skin tastes bad to predators

Red Toad

Lives in ponds and lakes; doesn't like sunshine; eats insects and spiders; skin has lots of bumps on it; males sing songs to attract females; females lay lots of eggs

Velvet Mite

Lives on the ground in forests; bodies are covered in red hair; eats termites for a tasty treat; bright red color tells predators not to eat them because they taste bad

Red Panda

Latin name translates to "shining cat;" lives in India and China; not many left in the world; good tree climber; has fur on bottom of feet (does your cat or dog?)

Orange

King Baboon Tarantula
Lives in African deserts; bites and hisses at predators; keeps cool by digging holes (burrows) and staying in them for months; has eight eyes!

Brush-Footed Butterfly
Walks on four legs instead of six; front legs are short and covered with hair; some species migrate to warm places in the winter; praying mantises like to eat them

Leaf Beetle
Eats lots of leaves; is hated by gardeners and farmers; comes in lots of colors and sizes; some have spot patterns; there are more than 40,000 different types (species)

Crawfish
Related to lobsters and spiders; some are pink or blue; also called a crawdaddy or mudbug; pinches fingers that try to pick it up

Cape Cobra
Lives in South Africa; has a forked tongue; comes in several colors; opens a "hood" on the sides of its head when threatened; likes to eat bird eggs and small animals

Goldfish
Favorite pet fish for kids; originally from China; likes warm, clean water

Orangutan
Found in Asian forests and zoos; lives in trees; sleeps in nests made from tree branches; loves fruit; makes rain hats from leaves; not many left in the world

Yellow

Tang Fish
Likes warm water near Hawaii and Japan; eats algae and ocean grass; turns brown and white at night; hangs onto rocks while sleeping; has small spines near its tail

Banded Moth Caterpillar
Larvae is covered in long hair; eats lots of leaves after turning into a caterpillar; uses poison in leaves to make itself poisonous to birds (cool trick, huh?)

Yellow Tree Frog
Lives in trees in Costa Rica; catches mosquitos and small fish with its sticky tongue; eats its skin after shedding; males sing loudly to attract females

Crab Spider
Has eight eyes and two pairs of extra-long front legs; sneaks up on its prey; can walk backward, sideways, and forward; hides on flower petals

Duck
Called a duckling when young; doesn't need to eat or drink for the first three days of its life; lives near water; follows mom everywhere; takes a while to learn to fly

Eyelash Viper
Lives in South American rain forests; has sharp fangs for injecting poison; hangs upside down by its tail; has scales over eyes which look like eyelashes

Yellow Butterfly
Flies fast, eats flower nectar during the day, takes sun baths, has colorful scales on its wings, starts life as a hungry caterpillar, orange spots look like eyes to predators

Green

Green Iguana
Climbs rocks and trees with long claws; has lots of pointy scales that look like horns down its back; tail has stripes; can grow taller (longer) than people!

Emerald Tree Boa
Tree-dwelling snake found in South American rain forests; eats birds and mice; looks friendly but still scares moms in zoos

Amazon Parrot
Lives in South and Central America; sings and talks a lot; can say bad words very well; not many left in the wild because their trees have been cut down and people want them for pets

Praying Mantis
Found all over America; follows prey with its big eyes; likes to eat other insects; might like to eat you!

Tomato Hornworm
Caterpillar that turns into a moth; has a red horn near its butt; disliked by farmers because it eats the stems and leaves off tomato plants

Tree Frog
Lives in trees in Central America; catches insects with its tongue; lays eggs on leaves over ponds; tadpoles hatch from eggs and fall into ponds; snakes like to eat their eggs

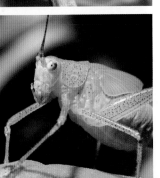

Katydid
Green body looks like leaves; males use their wings to sing love songs to females; the song sounds like "katy did, katy didn't" to people

Blue

Dragonfly
Has large eyes and small antennae; eats mosquitoes and other flying insects; can fly very fast; nymphs (young dragonflies) breathe air through their butts

Seahorse
Changes colors like a chameleon; uses tail to pick things up; lives near coral reefs and grass sea beds; swims with its head; males give birth to babies

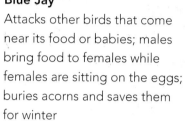

Blue Jay
Attacks other birds that come near its food or babies; males bring food to females while females are sitting on the eggs; buries acorns and saves them for winter

Chameleon
Name means "earth lion;" comes from Africa; tongue can be longer than its body; catches fast-moving bugs with the sticky tip on the end of its tongue

Common Blue Butterfly
Males are blue; females are brown; adults drink sweet nectar from flowers with tongues that work like straws; caterpillars are green with yellow stripes

Electric Blue Fish
Males are bright blue; females are brown or grey; moms carry eggs and newborn babies (called fry) in their mouths for three weeks; people keep them as pets in fish tanks

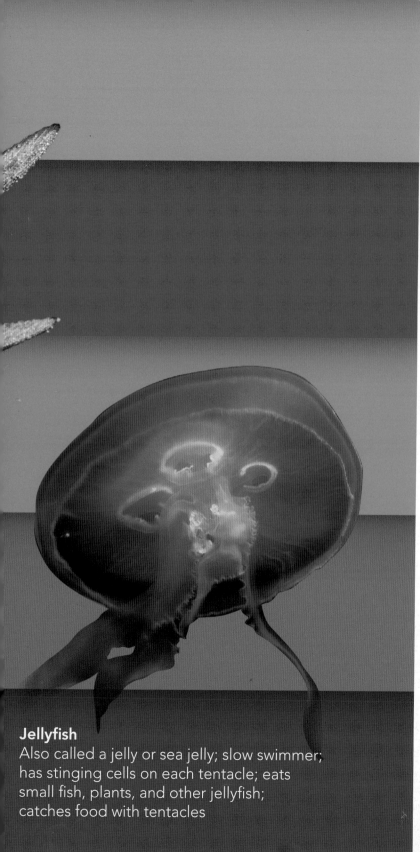

Jellyfish
Also called a jelly or sea jelly; slow swimmer; has stinging cells on each tentacle; eats small fish, plants, and other jellyfish; catches food with tentacles

Purple

Sea Urchin
Lives in oceans all over the world; close relative of the starfish; hangs onto rocks with hundreds of sticky feet; some have sharp spines and some have dull spines

Shore Crab
Lives near the edge of tidal pools; walks sideways; has polka dots on claw pinchers; uses pinchers the way we use our hands

Jellyfish
Comes in lots of colors — purple, orange, yellow, blue, red, and pink; has tentacles near its mouth; sometimes has stripes

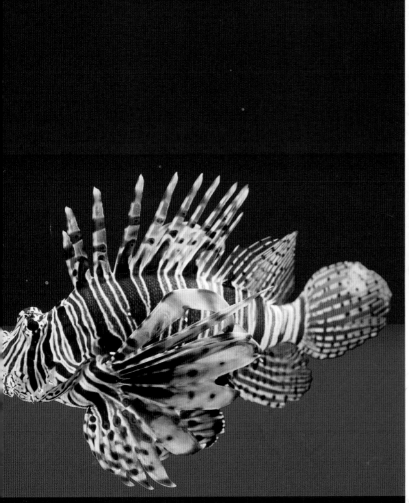

Sea Urchin Shell
Skeleton of sea urchin (far left); found with seashells on the beach and under water; raised bumps show where spines were; white spots show where tube feet were

Lionfish
Related to scorpion fish; has long spines on its fins; the tips of the spines have poison on them; has lots of stripes; chases prey into a corner and eats it in one big bite

Weevil
Type of beetle; comes in lots of colors; farmers and gardeners hate them because they eat the leaves of fruits and veggies

Rat Snake
Eats rats and birds; hunts at night; kills prey by squeezing it; smells the world with its tongue; plays dead when scared by people; is hated by bird lovers

Yellow and Orange

Sun Conure Parrot
Colors get brighter as the bird gets older; likes to eat fruit, berries, and flowers; makes a nice pet; scares people when it screams

Canary
Named after its home in the Canary Islands near Spain and Africa; has yellow feathers with an orange beak and feet; males sing more than females

Bearded Dragon
Type of lizard from Australia; eats insects and plants in the woods; has scales that look like spines around its face; looks scary but makes a nice pet

Lubber Grasshopper
Only lives about one year; has wings but can't fly; hisses and squirts bubbly poison at predators; birds and mammals puke if they eat it

Cleopatra Butterfly
Caterpillars have ten legs and lots of long hair; adults keep their wings closed most of the time; males are yellow with orange forewings; females are pale green

Yellow Paper Wasp
Makes nests from chewed-up wood mixed with spit; feeds caterpillars to its babies; males attack anything that disturb their nests; females hibernate like bears all winter

Orange Cup Coral
Lives in cold ocean water; has long tentacles with stinging cells for catching food; glues its body to a rock when small and stays there its whole life

Orange and Red

Garden Snail
Related to the sea snail; secretes a thick slime that helps it crawl over rough ground; uses tiny teeth on its tongue to scrape algae from rocks

Corn Snake
Also called red rat snake; often kept as a pet; named for the corn-like pattern on its belly; sleeps during the day; hunts for food at night

Discus Fish
Lives in the Amazon River in South America; also comes in green, red, brown, and blue; people like its bright colors in fish tanks

Shield Bug
Related to the bedbug and kissing bug; its antennae has five parts; sucks sap from plants for food with a beak-like mouth and tongue

Monarch Butterfly
Flies long distances (migrates) to spend the winter in California or Mexico; eats milkweed nectar for food; females lay their eggs under milkweed leaves

Box Turtle
Cools off by digging holes in the mud; males have bright red or orange eyes; females have brown eyes; hibernates under leaves in the winter; likes to eat garden snails

Rooster
Eats worms and bugs for a treat; pecks people and animals in its territory; knows when predators are sneaking up on it by sensing vibration

Red and Blue

Cinnabar Moth
Found in Europe and Asia; caterpillars are black with yellow stripes; caterpillars eat each other when they run out of leaves; adult moths taste bad to birds

American Kestrel
Small bird in the falcon family; looks for prey by flying in one place; males are colorful and females are brown; males impress females by diving from tall trees

Mandrill Monkey
Comes from Africa; related to baboons; lives in large groups; likes to eat leaves and insects; males have red and blue faces but females do not

Morpho Butterfly
Lives in rainforests in Central and South America; wings are shiny; drinks liquid from rotting fruit; closes its wings when it sleeps; its caterpillars are reddish brown and green

Rock Lizard
Lives in Africa; likes to eat termites and ants; females are brown; males are brown at night but turn red and blue during the day; males hit other males in the face with their tails

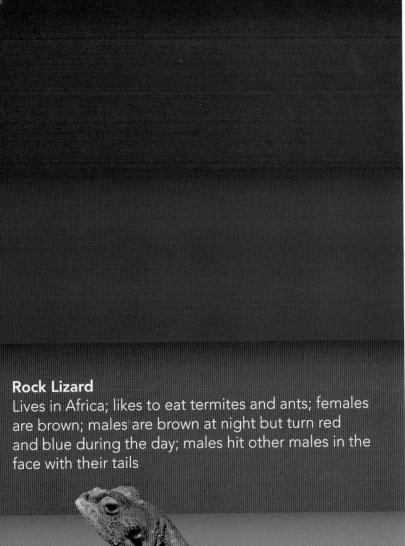

Wild Turkey
Likes to sleep in trees; males are called "gobblers" and females are called "hens;" females have white or gray heads; males have blue and red heads during mating season to attract females

Coral Hind Fish
Lives in the Red Sea near coral reefs; speckled with bright blue polka dots; gets clean by letting other fish eat parasites and algae off its scales

Blue and Green

Peacock
Brightly colored bird from India; males are called peacocks; females are called peahens; males have huge tails which fan out to impress females; females are gray or brown with small tails

Sea Anemone
Relative of jellyfish; lives in coral reefs; has lots of tentacles floating around its mouth; tentacles have stinging cells to catch food; lets clown fish hide between its tentacles

Blue Angelfish
Has a flat body; sometimes has a yellow tail; lives in coral reefs; eats jellyfish (without getting stung!); people like to keep them as pets in fish tanks

Boomslang Snake
Lives in Africa; is very poisonous; climbs trees to steal bird eggs; fun to see in a zoo; scary to see in the wild; females are brown; males are colorful

Snout Beetle
Named for its long, curved nose; also called a weevil; eats leaves and flowers; females use their long noses to dig holes for eggs; males have short noses

Violet-Ear Hummingbird
Lives in Central America; sucks nectar from flowers with a long tongue that comes out of its beak; males are more colorful than females and young birds

Anole Lizard
Also called the red-throated anole; males have throat pouches (called dewlaps); males show their dewlaps to impress females and to tell other males to go away

Black and White

Zebra
Lives in Africa; close relative of the horse;
stripes help it hide from lions and hyenas;
some scientists think the stripes also help
the zebra hide from blood-sucking parasites

Giant Panda
Lives in China; eats lots of bamboo; lives about 25 years; not many left in the world; has a big head and a short tail; has thick, waterproof fur; takes naps in trees

Crow
Eats lots of earthworms; steals food from friends; females build nests from sticks and mud; uses branches and sticks as a tool to find insects; hides extra food under leaves

Orca Whale
Also called killer whale; is the largest member of the dolphin family; is found in warm and cold oceans; families swim and hunt together; does tricks for tourists at marine parks

Dove
Beloved as a symbol of peace; is a close relative of the much-hated pigeon; makes soft cooing sounds; males and females make special milk for their newborn chicks

Snowy Owl
Lives in the cold Arctic; has feathers on its feet; all-white feathers get black spots and stripes in the summer; pants like a dog when hot to cool off

Dog
Related to wolves; likes to run after sticks and balls; cleans its fur with dirt; sweats through its tongue so it pants to cool off; looks snazzy in a red collar

Rainbow

Dogbane Beetle
Eats poisonous plants without getting sick; sprays acid from its butt onto animals or people who pick it up; skin colors shine in the light

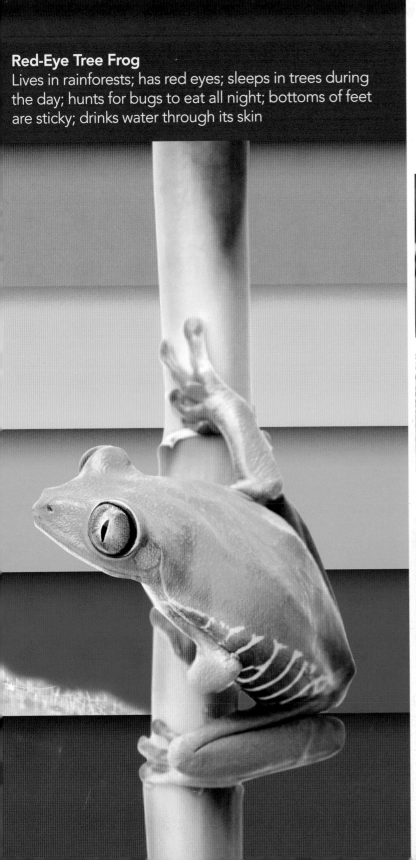

Red-Eye Tree Frog
Lives in rainforests; has red eyes; sleeps in trees during the day; hunts for bugs to eat all night; bottoms of feet are sticky; drinks water through its skin

Panther Chameleon
Lives in Madagascar; likes to take sunbaths in trees; grabs things with its tail; catches bugs with its sticky tongue; males are bigger and brighter than females

Rainbow Lorikeet
Type of parrot from Australia and Indonesia; has strong feet; lives in forests; sucks nectar from flowers for food; small hairs on the tip of its tongue help it get extra nectar

Locust
Also called long-horned grass-hopper; lives and flies with lots (sometimes millions!) of other locusts; hated by farmers and gardeners because it eats leaves off plants

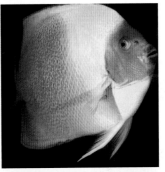

Angelfish
Lives in coral reefs; long fins help it swim fast; eats shrimp in the ocean; eats other angelfish in fish tanks; likes to play hide and seek

Toucan Bird
Lives in trees in Central and South America; beak has sharp, cutting edges like a knife; eats fruit, bugs, and eggs; talks a lot; toucan dads feed their babies

AND

Some animals have lots of color.

Some animals have none.

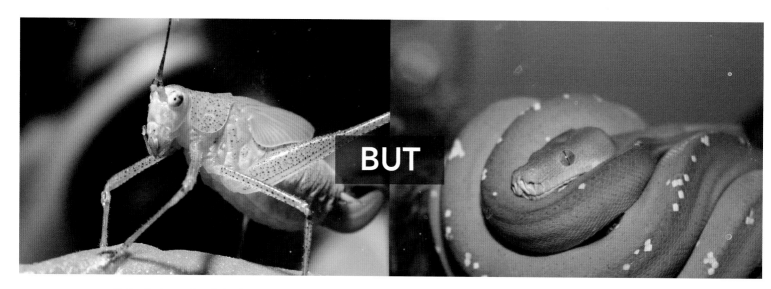

BUT

Color helps animals hide so other
animals don't eat them.

Color also helps animals hide so they can sneak
up on animals they want to catch and eat.

AND

Some animals — usually males — use color to get females to notice them.

Some animals use color to tell other animals to go away.

PLUS

Some animals change colors when they get hot or cold, or when they are scared or need to hide.

Other animals change colors as they age; they're one color as babies and another color as adults.

Colorful animals are fun to look at. Luckily for us, the world is full of them!

Index